ULIAQ'S Amazing Animals: Arctic Char

WRITTEN BY
Danny Christopher

ILLUSTRATED BY
Amiel Sandland

Hi! My name is Uliaq. I love animals. One of my favourite animals is the Arctic char. Arctic char are amazing!

3

Gills

Arctic char are fish. They use their fins and powerful tails to move in the water.

Arctic char use their gills to breathe underwater.

They grow to about 45 centimetres in length and can weigh up to 4.5 kilograms. But some Arctic char have been found that are much heavier!

45 cm

- - - - - - - - - - - - - - - -

4.5 kg

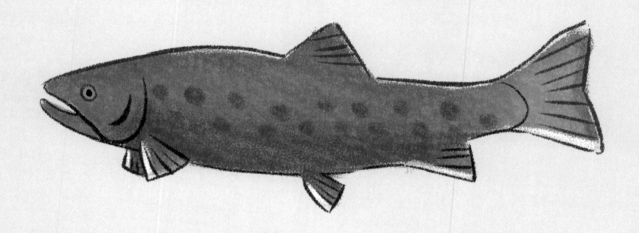

Their bellies are pale and their sides and back are greenish-grey. They have spots all over their bodies.

In the fall, their fins and bellies develop a bright orange colour, especially the males.

Let's look at the map!

Arctic char live mostly in cold northern waters around the Arctic. They are found in the ocean as well as in lakes and rivers.

12

Arctic char eat lots of different types of food. They eat snails, shrimp, and even other fish.

When it gets really cold, Arctic char eat zooplankton. Zooplankton are tiny animals that you need a microscope to see.

In the fall, Arctic char travel from the ocean to lakes and rivers to lay their eggs in gravel. One fish can lay up to 5000 eggs.

A female Arctic char lays eggs every two or three years. The baby Arctic char hatch in the spring.

I told you! Arctic char are amazing. That's why they are one of my favourite animals.

What do you like about Arctic char?